Good King Wenceslas

Good King Wenceslas

A Legend
in Music and
Pictures

Mary Reed Newland

THE SEABURY PRESS • NEW YORK

1980
The Seabury Press
815 Second Avenue, New York, N.Y. 10017

Printed in the United States of America

Library of Congress Cataloging in Publication Data
Newland, Mary, Reed
  Good King Wenceslas.

  1.   Wenceslaus, Saint, Duke of Bohemia, 907?-935?
  I.   Title.
BX4700.W4N4   783.6'52   80-36787
ISBN 0-8164-0474-7

Calligraphy by Anita Karl

To Benjamin and Erica
both born in Africa
(she the day after
the feast of Stephen)
who longed to see
"the snow lay round about
deep and crisp and even."

Introduction

Good King Wenceslas is one of the most popular carols — in fact, one of the most popular songs — ever written. The story of the saint about whom it was written and the talented and unusual man who wrote it are almost as much fun to know about as the carol is to sing.

First of all, although Wenceslas (?907-?935) was indeed very good, he was really not a king. John Mason Neale (1818-1866), the learned English scholar and hymnologist who created the carol, knew that Wencesla was not a king but felt, undoubtedly, that "king" was the easiest way to describe him. The fact is that Wenceslas was duke of Bohemia. Bohemia, which is now part of Czechoslovakia, was an independent state, a duchy, in the days of Wenceslas and for many years thereafter, and the traditional ruler was a duke. And although Neale knew a great deal about the life of the Bohemian saint, he really made up the story that the words of the carol tell as being typical of the kind of man Wenceslas was. The lovely medieval tune of "Good King Wenceslas" was based on an old Swedish folksong.

If you think about it, the story of our lives rarely begins with our birth. The story of Wenceslas actually begins with his grandmother. It begins with her because, unlike most people's grandmothers, she was to become a saint — St. Ludmilla.

In the year AD 874, Borivoi, duke of Bohemia, and his wife Ludmilla learned of Christ's message of love and peace, and were baptized into the Christian faith. Until then their home-land, Bohemia, had a harsh and cruel form of paganism as a religion. Many people believe that St. Methodius came to Bohemia to spread the Good News. He did not stop at baptizing the rulers — he baptized their whole court. But the old pagan religion was not dead. Despite the example set by Ludmilla and Borivoi and their household, many of the great Bohemian nobles kept their old religion and were suspicious of the new Christians.

Borivoi and Ludmilla had a son, Wratislaw. He was raised by his parents as a Christian. When he grew up he married a noblewoman called Drahomira. And the young couple had a son who they called Wenceslas. He would one day rule as duke of Bohemia. From the beginning, Wenceslas' grandmother Ludmilla took a great interest in the boy and had great plans for his future. And the most important part of her plan was that Wenceslas would be a good Christian ruler. Ludmilla was probably not convinced that her daughter-in-law Drahomira was a sincere, Christian, and so Ludmilla took over the education of her grandson herself — just to make sure he grew up the way she thought he should.

In the company of his devout grandmother and her chaplain young Wenceslas grew in love for God and grew in prayer and virtue, too. He was such a good student that some people said he could speak Latin as well as a bishop.

But tragedy struck the ruling family of Bohemia before Wenceslas was old enough to become duke. His father Wratislaw was killed in battle and his mother Drahomira took over the government. Ludmilla's worst fears were realized. Drahomira had not been a sincere Christian at all, and she began a government policy of repression directed at Bohemia's Christians. Ludmilla was horrified to see all the work she and her husband had done to bring Christianity to their people threatened. She advised her grandson Wenceslas to seize control of the government from his mother. Then Ludmilla fled to her castle at Tetin, where she planned to devote the rest of her life to prayer and service to the poor. But Drahomira was taking no chances. She was convinced that Wenceslas would not be able to take power from her without his grandmother's support. And so she sent two pagan nobles to Tetin and they murdered Ludmilla.

But Drahomira's wicked plot failed. Christian supporters of Ludmilla and Wenceslas drove her into exile. At twenty, Wenceslas became ruler of Bohemia, although his grandmother (who was already thought of as a saint) did not live to see it. True to her teaching, Wenceslas vowed his devotion to God's law and to the church, and promised to rule with justice and mercy. As a Christian, his first act was to pardon his mother Drahomira of her awful crime and allow her to come back to court.

Wenceslas was a new kind of ruler for his people. He was the first duke of Bohemia to base his political rule on the Christian faith. The people came to love him for his generosity, his concern for justice, and for the severity with which he punished those nobles who oppressed the people. His faith was also an integral part of his personal life. He spent long hours in prayer and his Psalter was dog-eared from frequent use.

But the good Wenceslas lived in savage times. Not everyone respected him. As far as his hard-bitten nobles were concerned, he was more suited to be a bishop than a temporal ruler. They were horrified when they learned he was willing to deal with the Germans, who were traditional enemies of the Bohemians. In fact, Wenceslas signed a treaty with the Germans to end fighting during one of their periodic invasions of his country. He made peace to avoid unnecessary bloodshed — not because he was afraid. But this action of the young ruler was a signal for his old enemies, led once more by his mother Drahomira and his own younger brother Boleslav, to try to end his life — and his reign.

Wenceslas always tried to attend church on the feast days of the saints. On September 27, 935, while visiting the city of his brother Boleslav, he went to celebrate the feast of Sts. Cosmas and

Damian. Legends tell us that Wenceslas had been warned that his life would be in danger after the church service was over, but he refused to pay any attention to the warnings. Instead, he proposed a toast to his court in honor of St. Michael, one of his favorite saints. The toast was this: "To St. Michael whom we pray to guide us to peace and eternal joy." Wenceslas then said his prayers and went to bed.

The next morning, as he was on his way to church, he met his brother. The ancient chronicles of Wenceslas report that the ruler greeted his brother lovingly, and thanked him for his hospitality. Boleslav is said to have answered Wenceslas by saying, "Yesterday I did my best to serve you fittingly, but *this* must be my service today." With those words, he struck Wenceslas with his sword. As the brothers struggled, other conspirators fell on Wenceslas and stabbed him. Dying, the good young ruler prayed, "May God forgive you for this deed, my brother."

People in Czechoslovakia and many other places, too, have always remembered Wenceslas. It was written of him that he "kept the faith, helping the wretched, feeding the hungry, clothing the naked, protecting widows and orphans, ransoming prisoners, and loving and caring for the rich and poor alike." When John Mason Neale set out to write a carol for the feast of St. Stephen which falls on December 26 his thoughts immediately went to Wenceslas. The feast of St. Stephen is the day when people in Neale's country, England, give gifts to the poor. And he saw other similarities between the two saints. So John Mason Neale, writing in the year 1853, created a new legend of Wenceslas in his lovely carol and helped keep the young ruler's example fresh for the people of our day.

In many countries, St. Ludmilla's feast is celebrated on September 16. St. Wenceslas is remembered on September 28 — and every time we sing John Mason Neale's carol "Good King Wenceslas."

Good King Wenceslas looked out
On the feast of Stephen,

When the snow lay round about,
Deep and crisp and even,

Brightly shone the moon that night,
Though the frost was cruel.

When a poor man came in sight
Gath'ring winter's fuel,

"Hither, page, and stand by me,
If thou knowst it, telling

"Yonder peasant, who is he?
Where and what his dwelling?"

"Sire, he lives a good league hence,
Underneath the mountain,

Right against the forest fence,
By St. Agnes fountain,"

"Bring me flesh and bring me wine,
Bring me pine logs hither.

Thou and I will see him dine
When we bear them thither."

Page and monarch, forth they went,
Forth they went together,

Through the rude wind's wild lament
And the bitter weather,

"Sire, the night is darker now,
And the wind blows stronger,

Fails my heart, I know not how
I can go no longer."

"Mark my footsteps, my good page,
Tread thou in them boldly,

Thou shalt find the winter's rage
Freeze thy blood less coldly,"

In his master's steps he trod,
Where the snow lay dinted,

Heat was in the very sod
     Which the saint had printed,

Therefore, Christian men, be sure,
Wealth or rank possessing,

Ye who now will bless the poor
Shall yourselves find blessing.

Good King Wenceslas

Text by John Mason Neale, 1853
Tune: Piae Cantiones, 1582
Harmonized by William F. Entriken, 1980

1

Good King Wenceslas looked out
On the Feast of Stephen,
When the snow lay round about,
Deep and crisp and even.
Brightly shone the moon that night,
Though the frost was cruel,
When a poor man came in sight
Gathering winter's fuel.

2

"Hither, page, and stand by me,
If thou knowst it, telling
Yonder peasant, who is he?
Where and what his dwelling?"
"Sire, he lives a good league hence,
Underneath the mountain,
Right against the forest fence,
By Saint Agnes' fountain."

3

"Bring me flesh and bring me wine,
Bring me pine-logs hither.
Thou and I will see him dine
When we bear them thither."
Page and monarch, forth they went,
Forth they went together,
Through the rude wind's wild lament
And the bitter weather.

4

"Sire, the night is darker now,
And the wind blows stronger.
Fails my heart, I know not how
I can go no longer."
"Mark my footsteps, my good page,
Tread thou in them boldly.
Thou shalt find the winter's rage
Freeze thy blood less coldly."

5

In his master's steps he trod,
Where the snow lay dinted.
Heat was in the very sod
Which the Saint had printed.
Therefore, Christian men, be sure,
Wealth or rank possessing,
Ye who now will bless the poor
Shall yourselves find blessing.